The Kid

by Michael Gow

CURRENCY PRESS
The performing arts publisher
www.currency.com.au

GRIFFIN THEATRE COMPANY

Principal Sponsor
PKF
Chartered Accountants
& Business Advisers

CURRENCY PLAYS

First published in 1983
by Currency Press Pty Ltd,
PO Box 2287, Strawberry Hills, NSW, 2012, Australia
enquiries@currency.com.au
www.currency.com.au
in association with
Nimrod Theatre Company, Sydney

Copyright © Michael Gow, 1983, 2008.

COPYING FOR EDUCATIONAL PURPOSES

The Australian *Copyright Act 1968* (Act) allows a maximum of one chapter or 10% of this book, whichever is the greater, to be copied by any educational institution for its educational purposes provided that that educational institution (or the body that administers it) has given a remuneration notice to Copyright Agency Limited (CAL) under the Act.

For details of the CAL licence for educational institutions contact CAL, 19/157 Liverpool Street, Sydney, NSW, 2000. Tel: (02) 9394 7600; Fax: (02) 9394 7601; E-mail: info@copyright.com.au

COPYING FOR OTHER PURPOSES

Except as permitted under the Act, for example a fair dealing for the purposes of study, research, criticism or review, no part of this book may be reproduced, stored in a retrieval system, or transmitted in any form or by any means without prior written permission. All enquiries should be made to the publisher at the address above.

Any performance or public reading of *The Kid* is forbidden unless a licence has been received from the author or the author's agent. The purchase of this book in no way gives the purchaser the right to perform the play in public, whether by means of a staged production or a reading. All applications for public performance should be addressed to the playwright c/- Shanahan Management, PO Box 1509, Darlinghurst NSW 2010; email admin@shanahan.com.au.

NATIONAL LIBRARY OF AUSTRALIA CIP DATA

Author:	Gow, Michael.
Title:	The kid / author, Michael Gow.
Edition:	Rev. ed.
Publisher:	Strawberry Hills, N.S.W.: Currency Press, 2008.
ISBN:	9780868198330 (pbk.)
Subjects:	Australian drama.
Dewey Number:	A822.3

Typeset by Dean Nottle for Currency Press.
Printed by Ligare Book Printers, Riverwood
Cover photograph by Olivia Martin-McGuire

The Kid received a workshop at the 1982 Australian National Playwrights' Conference, directed by Aubrey Mellor with Jack Hibberd as dramaturg. The actors were John Gregg, Peter Kingston, Lorna Lesley, Bill McCluskey, Garry McDonald, Julie McGregor and Linden Wilkinson.

It was first performed in a revised version at the Winter Theatre, Fremantle, on 25 August 1983, with the following cast:

DONALD	Chris Bowes
SNAKE	Caroline McKenzie
ASPRO	Alan Charlton
DEAN	Nigel Devenport
DESIREE	Polly Low
THE WOMEN	Claire Haywood, Michelle Marzo
THE MEN	Ingle Knight

Director, Cesare C. Coli
Lighting Designer, Stewart Carter
Dramaturgy, George Tsousis

CHARACTERS

DONALD, 17
SNAKE, 18
ASPRO, 19
DEAN, 17
DESIREE, 15
WOMAN A, a country cafe proprietor
MAN A, a bookshop proprietor
WOMAN B, an apartment block caretaker
MAN B, Desiree's father
WOMAN C, distraught and middle-class
WOMAN D, in the Department of Social Services
MAN C, her husband

SETTING

The present. On the road from the North to Sydney and various locations around the city.

SCENE ONE

A country cafe.

DONALD *sits staring into space.* WOMAN A, *the proprietor, is cleaning up.*

WOMAN A: I have to tell someone. I have these terrible dreams. It's probably these westerlies. I dream about Peter, my husband. Can I tell you? Peter and his brother Phil were crop-dusters. They were doing well. One day Phil's plane clipped some trees on Robie's place and hit their barn. Burnt. The very next week I was getting tea and there was this tearing noise. I went to the back door and stood there as Peter's plane sailed over the house and landed in next door's dam. He was drowned, officially. They always flew so low. Twelve years ago this month. I dream I'm getting tea and it starts to rain. I can hear it on the roof. I know what it is, that's the awful thing. I know, even while I'm dreaming. But I go to the door saying: 'Good. We could do with the rain.' I get to the door and see it's Peter in little pieces falling slowly to the ground.

    Silence.

It's very quiet.
DONALD: When was it ever loud here?
WOMAN A: Nineteen fifty-two. Before the bypass. This town was a resort then. The main street was criss-crossed with coloured lights all summer. On New Year's Eve we all stood in the street and held hands and cried like on VE Night.
DONALD: You look very tired.
WOMAN A: Doesn't your mother worry you stay out so late?
DONALD: No.
WOMAN A: Another cuppa chino?
DONALD: No thanks.
WOMAN A: I'm happy to make it.
DONALD: No, really.
WOMAN A: You really don't have to go.
DONALD: I'm happy to stay.

    SNAKE *enters.*

SNAKE: Are you open for business or what?
WOMAN A: Yes, my girl. I'm open for business.
SNAKE: Marvellous. [*She goes out and screams.*] It's okay, Dean! She's open for business! [*She comes back in.*] Was this town designed by a moron or what? There's one other milk bar right up the other end of the street and it's closed.
WOMAN A: May I help you?
SNAKE: Where's the shithouse?
WOMAN A: I beg your pardon?
SNAKE: You do have one? Or do you spread it on toast and call it paté? That's what I reckon they do in them coffee shops. Makes you sick, a milk bar's a milk bar.

> DEAN *and* ASPRO *enter.*

Sit down, Pro, and annoy this nice young man. This is Aspro. He lives on them. That's our brother Dean. I'm called Snake but my name's Yvonne.
WOMAN A: Can I help any of you young people?
SNAKE: Three cupsa chino. Through here?

> SNAKE *goes out, followed by* WOMAN A.

ASPRO: When she turned sixteen Auntie Eileen sent her upstairs with a wharfie. When she came down she said, 'Christ, it was like a snake'. [*He laughs.*] Cuppa chino?
DONALD: Er...
ASPRO: [*shouting to the kitchen*] Make that four! What's your name?
DONALD: Um...
ASPRO: That's unusual. Foreign? Or a nickname? Um short for... Bum. Oo-waaa.
DONALD: Donald.
ASPRO: Um short for Donald, I don't see the connection.
DONALD: Just Donald.
ASPRO: Just Donald? Have you got a complex or something? You must stop running yourself down. Is this the menu?
DONALD: That's right.
ASPRO: I hate plastic. Now let's see. Mmm. Yum.
DEAN: Hot, eh?
DONALD: Sorry.
DEAN: Hot. Don't you reckon?

DONALD: I suppose it is.
DEAN: Good.

> *He winks at* DONALD.

ASPRO: Hey, there's no prices on this menu. Is it all free?
DONALD: Nearly everything's off.
ASPRO: God! Fancy giving away your old food.
DEAN: I wouldn't mind a swim right now.
DONALD: Oh?
DEAN: What do you reckon?
DONALD: Oh, yes.
DEAN: Just strip off. A swim in the raw, eh? Nice?
DONALD: I…
DEAN: Yeah?

> *He winks again.*

ASPRO: I might try the pies. What do you think?
DONALD: Yes.
ASPRO: You had them?
DONALD: Probably.
DEAN: Fuck, it's hot.
ASPRO: I'll give it a go. *Hey! Bring us a pie! Thanks!* Bit quiet. Here.

> *He turns on a radio full blast.* SNAKE *comes back.*

SNAKE: That's better. You want to go? Aspro? Do you want to go? Turn that off.
ASPRO: Leave it.
SNAKE: Turn it off. Do you want to drive us all crazy or what?

> *She turns it off.*

ASPRO: Just because you hate music.
SNAKE: Shut up. We're on our way to Sydney. Pro was the victim of this terrible accident. He fell under a Randwick bus. He's been going downhill ever since.
ASPRO: My actual brain's not impaired.
SNAKE: He's going to pieces. There's no obvious reason, so there's no cure.

> WOMAN A *re-enters.*

WOMAN A: Four cupsa chino. Pie. Anything else?
DONALD: Umm…

ASPRO: Make that four. Four ums. [*Laughing*] See, I haven't lost my sense of humour, despite this. That will be all. You may go.
SNAKE: And then there's the Other Thing.
ASPRO: The Other Thing. [*To the* WOMAN] You may go.

    WOMAN A *goes*.

SNAKE: He hears voices.
ASPRO: Like Joan of Arc.
SNAKE: No saint ever used language like this. We've been threatened twice with indecent language. He's getting to be a liability.
ASPRO: This bloke keeps yelling things at me. Filthy things. So I have to fight back.
SNAKE: He had an attack in this Golden Fleece cafeteria yesterday. The old cheese behind the counter shat herself.

    ASPRO *laughs*.

ASPRO: I can't help it.
SNAKE: Poor Aspro. Oh, this coffee's ratshit. Anyway, we're on our way to Sydney to claim the compensation. It's taken so long. Things like that always take forever.

    DEAN *throws sugar cubes at* DONALD.

Especially when you come from where we do. As far as the turds who run things are concerned the world ends at Hornsby. Look, give me that. Honestly.

    She cuts up Aspro's pie.

You have to treat him like cut glass. That's not easy driving all the way to Sydney and back every time the Department finds another excuse to keep us waiting. But this is the last time. I've got this letter. It's in my bag. What a day it'll be. I got a new dress for the last interview. And I ripped a handbag off from the Fosseys in Coffs.
DEAN: So hot.
SNAKE: We really should get going. Someone might recognise the car. Finish your cuppa chino, Pro.
ASPRO: What about me pie?
SNAKE: Take it with you. Now hurry up.
ASPRO: This coffee's ratshit.
SNAKE: He can't think for himself. Can you?
ASPRO: My actual brain's not impaired.
SNAKE: Don't whinge.

ASPRO: I don't whinge.
SNAKE: You whinge, trust me.
DEAN: [*to* DONALD] You got a job?
DONALD: I work in the bookshop across the street.
DEAN: Like it?
DONALD: It's all right.
SNAKE: Oh, Dean, come on.
DEAN: Do you like your job?
SNAKE: He hates it, now come on.
DONALD: It's not bad.
ASPRO: Ha ha.
SNAKE: Come on.
ASPRO: Don't whinge.
SNAKE: Here we go.
DEAN: What about the boss?
DONALD: He's all right.
DEAN: You should hate him. You should always hate the boss.
DONALD: Why?
DEAN: What's he like?
DONALD: Strange. He's an intellectual, I suppose. He writes a column in the local paper.
DEAN: An intellectual? And he lives here?
DONALD: He used to live in Perth but it was too Philistine, he said. He wants to make this his own Lake Isle of Innisfree.
ASPRO: We've been there.
SNAKE: Have not.
ASPRO: Have so. It's near Nambucca Heads, isn't it?
DONALD: No.
SNAKE: Ha ha.
DEAN: The work hard?
DONALD: Not really. Business isn't good. This place has had it. They put a bypass in. It's really dead. A few schoolteachers retire here.
DEAN: Hell on earth.
DONALD: And our shop's very specialised. We sell books that should never have been published. He thinks it's civilised but they don't sell.
DEAN: But you like it?
DONALD: I was lucky to get a job after school. The atmosphere's nice. I play records.

DEAN: Opera?
DONALD: Yes.
DEAN: I knew it.

> WOMAN A *enters*

WOMAN A: I have to close up.
SNAKE: Come on, Dean. We have to go.
ASPRO: You've said that.
WOMAN A: I have to close up.
DEAN: You are closed up.
SNAKE: Bags sitting in the front.
ASPRO: Ohhh! I want to.
SNAKE: I said it first. You're too slow.
ASPRO: Of course I'm too slow. My handicap should be taken into account.
SNAKE: Too late. Besides, you fart.

> SNAKE *and* ASPRO *go out.*

WOMAN A: Well, I'm going to put the lights out.

> *She leaves the bill and goes.*

DEAN: I've got my eye on you. Noticed? [*He lights the bill with a cigarette lighter.*] In a word, I'd say—pathetic.

> *The lights go out.*

You've been watching me too. When a bloke looks at my jeans first instead of at Snake I know what I might be up against.

> *A car horn is heard offstage.*

Come with us. Come to Sydney.
SNAKE: [*offstage*] Carn, Dean!
DEAN: Be a man. Come with us. You don't have to say anything. I'll wait for you in the car. Whatever happens, I'm your friend.

> DEAN *exits.* WOMAN A *re-enters.*

WOMAN A: All right? [*Seeing they have left without paying*] Pests.

SCENE TWO

The bookshop.
DONALD *is unpacking books from a carton.* MAN A *leafs through one.*

MAN A: [*reading*] 'These lavishly illustrated, exquisitely bound volumes will be a most valuable addition to any thinking person's shelves. The comprehensive text, compiled'—listen to this—'by some of our country's leading historians, will give hours of fascinating reading. The colour plates, selected by respected art experts, will provide a breathtaking view of our nation's colourful beginnings. This is a veritable guided tour through the wonder that was colonial Australia.' Oh, look at this! And this! Unbelievable. See this?
DONALD: Yes.
MAN A: Isn't that—My God.
DONALD: They weigh a ton.
MAN A: Worth every cent. I'll look us up. [*He leafs through the back of the book.*] Here we are. Two-three-seven. There we are. Look at that!
DONALD: The railway station.
MAN A: Isn't that wonderful? My God. This is deeply moving. Smell them.

They do.

Mmm. The smell of a fresh masterpiece. My God. And look. Over the page. The Henty-Jones property. Isn't it a fine building? Look at the verandahs. How'd you like to sit there at sunset, eh? Eh? With a whisky, watching your cows come home, building a new society? Eh? We get three and a half pages. They start with Oxley, then the squatters. That's when the Henty-Jones place went up. Apparently his wife was First Fleet. They've got a coat of arms over the fireplace. There's the clearing of the land. How'd you like to chop one of them down before breakfast, eh? Eh? There's Danny McReady, after they tracked him down. No white man was a match for those black trackers. Oh, and there's the convict gangs building the road. And then the railway coming. Those wild Irish navvies. Marvellous times. Marvellous times. Aren't you proud? You should memorise every line of this. It took four years to produce. This is your past. You wait till we build our historic village. Then you'll see, then you'll see. History? Let's have a drink.
DONALD: It's only half past nine.
MAN A: It's never too early to toast the birth of a nation.

> MAN A *goes out. Silence.* DONALD *sits on the floor and leafs through the book.* DEAN *comes in silently. Pause.*

DEAN: I'm not going to beg.
DONALD: What!
DEAN: I said I'm not going to beg.
DONALD: That's a relief.
DEAN: You were waiting for me to come back and drag you out.
DONALD: No.
DEAN: No?
DONALD: No.
DEAN: Well, where were you?
DONALD: Where I always am.
DEAN: Don't get smart.
DONALD: Sorry.
DEAN: I'm not very popular because of this.
DONALD: That's not my problem.
DEAN: Are you happy?
DONALD: What?
DEAN: You don't look happy.
DONALD: Why should I?
DEAN: Coward.
DONALD: That's right.
DEAN: Don't brag about it.
DONALD: Or you'll what?
DEAN: You make me chuck.
DONALD: Pathetic.
DEAN: You said it.
DONALD: Pathetic.
SNAKE: [*offstage*] *Are you coming or what?!*
DEAN: No.
SNAKE: [*offstage*] *I'll send Aspro in!*
DEAN: [*to* DONALD] He'll love it.
DONALD: You're a real daredevil.
DEAN: I know you wanted to come. Didn't you?
DONALD: It was late. I was tired.
DEAN: You must have.
DONALD: I was bored.
DEAN: You wanted it real bad. And you still do.
DONALD: You can see my innermost secrets.
DEAN: I can look right through you.

THE KID

ASPRO *comes in, radio blaring.*

ASPRO: Snake says you have to come right away.
DONALD: Turn that down.
DEAN: Who are you talking to?
DONALD: Him.
DEAN: Who?
DONALD: Could you please ask him to turn the radio off or down?
DEAN: Who?
DONALD: [*turning the radio off*] Your brother.
DEAN: You're treading a thin line.

MAN A *comes back with a bottle and glasses.*

MAN A: Good morning to you. Can I help you?
DONALD: We don't have what they want.
DEAN: We're just browsing, thanks.
MAN A: Anything in particular? Fiction? *Campfire Yarns*? *Down the Emu Trail*? *Stockyard Stories*? Great stuff. I collected it from the contributions to the 'Voice of Yesterday' column I have in the local paper. I just sit the old-timers down, buy them a drink and let them wander back through their lives. The stuff that comes out! They have an amazingly rich culture all of their own. It's marvellous.
DEAN: Must be.
ASPRO: They got pictures in them?
DEAN: You'd better check.
ASPRO: Yes. No. [*He throws it away.*] No. [*Throwing the rest away*] No. No. No. No. No. No. These are terrible books. I prefer pictures. And the print needs to be pretty bold.

DONALD *picks the books up while the* MAN *goes on*. DONALD *silently urges* DEAN *to go*. DEAN *winks and turns to the* MAN.

MAN A: There's a wealth of historical stuff. National and local. I've done my own history of the area. An abridged version has just come out in this new work. I'm very pleased with it over all. Or verse? You like poetry? No greater medium for the expression of our, shall I say, heroic beginnings. *Anzacs and Eagles*. [*Pause.*] Marvellous stuff.
DEAN: Yeah.
MAN A: *Bush Ballads*. A classic.
DEAN: I'll say.
MAN A: You from around here?
DEAN: Nup.

MAN A: I thought your face was familiar.
DEAN: Could be.
MAN A: Do you ride?
DEAN: A bit.
MAN A: I might have seen you around the rodeo. You been on the rodeo circuit?
DEAN: Not really.
MAN A: Marvellous event. Folk culture.
DEAN: Dead set?
MAN A: I'll bet you shoot. I'll bet you're a great marksman, eh? Eh?
DEAN: Not bad.
MAN A: I could tell. With your mates. At night. Driving back at dawn with your kill. I can see it, I can see it. Here, this one:
> [*Reading*] 'Gaps are many at times, alas,
> War is heavy on life and limb,
> And many a weary day will pass
> Before a man replaces him.
> A man with a smile upon his face
> That ever is welcome around the place.'

A lament for a great time now vanished. Can I show you something, er, er…?
DEAN: Dean.
MAN A: Can I show you something, Dean?
DEAN: Sure.
MAN A: I've been asked to write a little play on the history of the town. One of the great characters was Danny McReady. Our own bushranger. Great man. Sums up the spirit of what it was that built this country. Would you look at it for me? Just to see how it reads?
DEAN: Unreal.
DONALD: Can you read?
MAN A: I'll just get it. This is marvellous.

> MAN A *goes*.

DONALD: Will you get lost!
DEAN: Nice bloke.
DONALD: Just go.
DEAN: Shithouse books, eh?
ASPRO: Reckon. Hey, that pie I had was right off. Is there a toilet around here?

DONALD: No.
DEAN: No? What a dump. Hey, what a dump! No dunny!
DONALD: Shut up. It's through there.
ASPRO: You're a mate.

    ASPRO *goes out.*

DONALD: Please. Go.
DEAN: Nup. No way.
DONALD: What have I done?
DEAN: Not a thing.

    SNAKE *comes in.*

SNAKE: Well, hello. Remember me? Your long lost sister? Long time no see. If you're not in that car and behind the wheel by the time I count ten—Where's Aspro?
DEAN: Guess.
SNAKE: One, two, three…
DEAN: Read a book. Improve your mind.
SNAKE: Four, five…
DEAN: Try this one. Here.

    Pause.

SNAKE: If I read it can we go?
DEAN: We'll see.
SNAKE: [*reading*] 'On the crimson breast of the sunset
    The Gray Selections lie
    And their lonely, grief-stained faces
    Are turned to a pitiless sky;

    MAN A *comes in.*

    They are wrinkled and seamed with drought-fire
    And wound at the throat with weeds,
    They sob in the aching loneness
    But never a passer heeds.'
MAN A: Lovely, lovely.
SNAKE: Now let's go. Where's Aspro?
DONALD: Out the back.
MAN A: This is it. It's quite short.
SNAKE: [*shouting*] *Aspro? You all right?!*
ASPRO: [*offstage*] *Oh yeah, I s'pose!*

MAN A: He wore his own armour. I thought if we put this over your head, to get the effect. On the actual day we'd have a slit here.

He puts a rubbish bin over DEAN's *head*

It's quite clean.

SNAKE: That's where he belongs.

DEAN: [*from inside the bin*] Watch your mouth.

MAN A: Can you see the words down here?

DEAN: Just.

MAN A: Right.

DEAN: [*reading*] 'This is a hard land, a cruel land. A land of savage beauty. A land of dry bones beneath a bleaching sun. It will be hard to win, but win it will. We will struggle against the elements: fire, wind, flooding rain and searing endless drought, to build here a land of free men, of proud tall men…'

SNAKE: Aspro?

ASPRO: [*offstage*] *Yeah, righto!*

DEAN: 'free of the yoke…' [*He makes vomiting noises.*] Good thing I've got this bin. Oh, Christ I'm crook.

More noises.

MAN A: It's not quite right yet.

DEAN: I'm going to die. Let me out.

MAN A: It's not exactly the final form.

DEAN: I'm going, I'm going.

More noises.

MAN A: You're right, you're right. It's no good. It's no good.

DEAN: [*taking the bin off his head*] So this is what intellectuals write. Load of shit. I wipe my arse of intellectuals.

He does so, with the script.

MAN A: It's rubbish, I know. But it's not my fault.

ASPRO *enters with some magazines.*

ASPRO: I made a bit of a mess. Sorry. I found these. They're amazing.

MAN A: They're special orders. Give them here.

ASPRO: What's a cock ring?

MAN A: They're for private customers…

ASPRO: [*reading*] 'Felicity continued working his cock and Jim felt the cum inside straining to blow. His hand reached up and gently stroked the back of the girl's neck—'

MAN A: Give that to me.

ASPRO: No, I want to see how it ends. [*Reading*] 'She took the hint and moved her hand away from Jim's tool, at the same time bringing her mouth down over it.' Oh, yuck.

MAN A: They are private orders. Give that to me. [*To* SNAKE] Business is slow. I have to meet a need or else. I've got an ulcer. [*To* DEAN] You're so right, it's awful. But it's what Mrs Booth wanted, something solid, something strong. A link with the past, she kept saying. She's an incredible woman. See, she has her photo here in the local history I did. It got good reviews. Here. Her ancestors were on the First Fleet.

DEAN: Granddad a convict, eh? What was he up for? Kiddie fucker, from the look of her.

SNAKE: [*to* ASPRO] Put that down and go to the car. Dean?

DEAN: [*throwing books into the bin*] That's where they belong. What sort of shop are you running, anyway? Lousy books. Selling filth.

DONALD: [*to the* MAN] I'm very sorry.

DEAN: [*seizing* DONALD *by his shirt front*] Don't you apologise for me. [*To the* MAN] And what about the staff? Do you call employing cocksuckers any way to run a business? Come on, we're off. Stop wasting time, you silly bitch, and get in the car.

SNAKE: Come on, Aspro. Out!

ASPRO: At least this stuff's got pictures.

    SNAKE *and* ASPRO *exit*.

DEAN: [*still holding* DONALD] You're lucky I don't burn this place to the ground.

    They go. MAN A *stands silent for a while. He goes to the bin and takes out a book. He leafs slowly through it.*

SCENE THREE

Open country. A car.

ASPRO *is asleep in the back.* SNAKE *in the front.* DONALD *watches* DEAN *piss. He finishes and beckons* DONALD, *who then gets out of the car.* DEAN *points to where* DONALD *should sit. They both sit.*

DEAN: Wishing you hadn't come?

DONALD: I'm sorry I let myself be dragged away.

DEAN: You didn't need much of a drag.

DONALD: I haven't got any things.
DEAN: You don't need things.
DONALD: I could never go back.
DEAN: Are you sorry you left that?
DONALD: I might be.
DEAN: Well, piss off. Go on. Hitch a ride back. Might even get a fuck as a bonus. Go on. Pathetic. No, I won't let you go. I know what you need.
DONALD: What?
DEAN: Tell you a story. 'Sharing is the basis of a good relationship.' Snake read that out to us out of *New Idea*. First fuck. I was eleven. She was twenty. Superb woman. She was engaged to our local Tae Kwon Do instructor. I was his star pupil. When she met me she broke off the engagement. She gave back the ring. He wasn't too happy about that. He thought he'd get me in a late-night ambush. I found out about it through a network of friends. One night at class I forgot to hold back and attacked with full force. His pelvis was shattered. There was this midnight mercy dash to the city. We all celebrated—she, me and a few close friends—by each drinking a bottle of Brandevino at the drive-in. Sick? We nearly died. Her ex was on his back for seven months. The Italians have a saying: 'Revenge is a dish that tastes sweetest when served cold.' Now. How old?
DONALD: Seventeen.
DEAN: Where?
DONALD: In a house.
DEAN: Whose house?
DONALD: The other person's.
DEAN: Name?
DONALD: Keith. He was a teacher. English History. He gave acting classes too sometimes. We did plays. *The Importance of Being Earnest*, *The Mikado*. And he gave private coaching. Poetry, novels.
DEAN: Did he like opera?
DONALD: Yes.
DEAN: This schoolteacher asked me home for coaching once. He said he might be able to get me through some test. He'd seen me playing basketball stripped. He offered me coffee. I said, 'I don't drink coffee'. What happened?
DONALD: I went to his place for coaching. Thomas Hardy. He got embarrassed and started speaking really softly. I could hardly hear him.

I just smiled and nodded. He opened his trousers and stood next to me. I just sat there.

DEAN: Dick in ear.

DONALD: [*laughing*] Dick in ear. And he kept saying, 'I've had so many sleepless nights, so many sleepless nights'. Then he played some records for me.

DEAN: Opera?

DONALD: Opera. Not much, is it? He taught me about the good things: art, poetry, good food, theatre.

DEAN: Opera.

DONALD: [*laughing*] Opera.

DEAN: First flush, eh, down the toilet of love? Since?

> DONALD *shrugs.*

A lot of dirty hankies and long showers.

> DONALD *laughs.*

I'm going to show you something. [*He rolls up his sleeve to reveal a tattoo.*] What does it say?

DONALD: 'Born to Die'.

DEAN: It's the greatest secret, right? No one else knows. If anyone found out I'd be dead. Once you've got this on you you're never free. I'll never lead a normal life. I'd never get a job. Bosses pretend to be respectable but they all know what I went through to earn this, what I stole, what I maimed, what colour holes I had to lick. A secret, right? Kiss me. Here.

> DONALD *kisses him on the cheek.*

You're like a brother. I'd die for you.

SNAKE: Oh, who flung dung? God Almighty. Aspro. Aspro!

ASPRO: Good one, eh?

SNAKE: Have you got a dead camel up your bum or what?

ASPRO: I need to go.

SNAKE: *Dean! Your brother needs to go poo-poo!*

DEAN: I'm coming.

SNAKE: Don't get snappy. We'd have been there by now.

DEAN: Come on. Out.

ASPRO: It's not my fault. It's not my fault.

DEAN: Shut up.

ASPRO: I'll do it in me pants. Then you'll be sorry.

DEAN: I'll beat it out of you if you don't shut up.

    DEAN *and* ASPRO *go.*

SNAKE: Honestly. I hate this trip. It's always chaos. Always a fight. By the time we get to Auntie Eileen's no one's talking to anyone. I have to do everything. Get the boys ready. Stock up on drinks and Marlboro and chips. Hate it. Won't it be great when we get the money? We'll be happy. We might take over a service station. Dean can fool around with his engines. I'll cook snacks and Pro can man the pumps. I'll have to help him with the change. I'll look back on all this and laugh. Hate it. All the people we end up taking along. Dean always collects someone.

DONALD: I see.

SNAKE: You must have been the first one ever to turn him down. He was that upset. He was driving like a maniac. He just drove over the median strip and back we came. Little turd. Know why he got chucked out of school? Mrs Tucker—guess what Dean called her—was wrapped in him. She used to beat shit out of him, for any reason, no reason, just so she could grab hold of him and whack his bum. One day he'd had enough and he told her to go and see one of the Abo stockmen and he'd fix her up. Poor woman grabbed all the rulers in the room and laid into Dean. He stood up, gave her a right hook and she went down like a ton of bricks. We all stood on the desks and cheered. I reckon Dean would win wars single-handed. The enemy would come to him on bended knees. People will do anything just to get a wink or a smile that says he likes you. Little turd. Foul temper. Lazy. But who cares when it's Dean?

    DEAN *and* ASPRO *re-enter.*

DEAN: What's the time?
SNAKE: I don't know.
DEAN: Then try the radio, shit face.

    She does. Music.

SNAKE: Ohh, yuck.
DEAN: Opera.
DONALD: Wagner.
DEAN: Chuck us a drink, Snake. [*To* DONALD] Can you drive?
DONALD: Not really.
DEAN: You do or you don't.

DONALD: I don't actually have a licence.
DEAN: Licence? A mere scrap of paper not fit to wipe a copper's arse. And that's low. I'm tired. You have the honour of driving us into the big smoke.

He opens a can he's been shaking.

ASPRO: Can I have a can?
SNAKE: No, you'll chuck.
ASPRO: Will not.
SNAKE: You did last time.
ASPRO: I won't. Tell her, Dean.
SNAKE: I am not having you spew down my neck.
ASPRO: Ooohhh, I will not.
SNAKE: No way.
DEAN: All right. All right.

He hands cans around.

[*To* DONALD] Now drive, gorgeous. Commonwealth Street. Know it? Auntie Eileen says it was always handy having the Children's Courts so handy. *Now drive!*
ALL: *Commonwealth Street! Yaa-a-y!*

Beer everywhere. Wind. The city appears in splendour at the back.

SCENE FOUR

A small flat, no more than a box with doors. Table, chairs, wardrobe.

WOMAN B *stands in the doorway with a large carton.* DESIREE *stands at the door blocking her entrance.* MAN B, *Desiree's father, lours in a corner of the room.*

WOMAN B: I brought this down. It was blocking the entrance.
DESIREE: Thank you.
WOMAN B: Hello, there.
DESIREE: He's very busy.
WOMAN B: Of course. It's very heavy. Do you need the stamps?
DESIREE: No.
WOMAN B: You're sure?
DESIREE: Yes. Here. Take them.
WOMAN B: Thank you very much. Nephew. American stamps are very different, aren't they?

DESIREE: They're American.

WOMAN B: It's not junk mail, is it? You've had a few, I've noticed. You do when you have a large structure like this in your care. I answered a questionnaire once. I thought it was about the elections on TV. A week later all this stuff arrived in the mail. How I could revolutionise myself. Well, first of all, why should I? No one would know me anymore—my family, kiddies. Then, why should I change? I am what I am. I wrote back to these people, telling them I didn't want any more of their garbage through the mail. But it kept coming. How I could improve my life. How can you improve life? So I kept sending the stuff back but they kept sending more. Letters from this chap who ran the place, this group. They weren't real letters, Mervyn held them up to the light and you could see they were roneoed. So I sent them back, saying we weren't at this address anymore. But they sent these forms for forwarding addresses and post office box numbers. Mervyn wrote and told them we'd been killed in a car accident.

DESIREE: There's no problem.

WOMAN B: He'll love the stamps.

WOMAN B goes. DESIREE eagerly opens the carton.

DESIREE: They're the new pamphlets. See? 'The Russian Threat Revealed in the Book of Daniel', 'Why God Chose the English Language', 'Intellectuals—God's Curse on Weak Rulers'. And some new 'Introductory Leaflets'. 'Dear Neighbour, I'd just like a few minutes of your precious time to tell you of God's wonderful Message.' I'll get rid of them straight away. What about the others? Do you want to look at them first? What'll we do with them?

The MAN goes to hit her.

I'm sorry. You were thinking, I'm sorry.

The MAN grabs some pamphlets from her. She goes back to the carton.

There are some more kits. Such a waste. People don't want to know. Just think, these were packed in America. We haven't watched one for a while. I wish I could work them. The slides are so good. So true. I'll get rid of these. I'll be gone fifteen minutes.

The MAN checks his watch.

Don't worry. I'll be back.

DESIREE goes. The MAN looks at a pamphlet, then throws it away.

SCENE FIVE.

A living room: settee, stereo, TV, door to the street.

WOMAN C *vacuums the floor listening to the end of* Madama Butterfly. *She is weeping. She sips a drink as she works. She finishes, takes the vacuum cleaner out, returns, tidies the settee. She stands, drinking, listening to the music, weeping. The music ends. She sits on the settee and takes out a bottle of pills.*

WOMAN C: Oh, Colin. You bastard.

    Knocking is heard.

SNAKE: [*offstage*] Auntie Eileen? Hello. It's me.
WOMAN C: Who's that?
SNAKE: [*offstage*] Hello.
WOMAN C: Sent someone to make sure?
SNAKE: [*offstage*] You there?
WOMAN C: [*swallowing a pill*] What a coward. A lousy note. Notice to quit. I quit.
SNAKE: [*offstage*] Auntie Eileen?
WOMAN C: Oh, leave me alone.
SNAKE: [*offstage*] Hello?
WOMAN C: Leave me alone!
SNAKE: [*offstage, through the letter opening*] Who's that?
WOMAN C: *Go away!*
SNAKE: [*offstage, through the letter opening*] Who is it?
WOMAN C: I don't need help.
SNAKE: [*offstage, through the letter opening*] Who are you?
WOMAN C: Oh, Colin.

    She takes another pill.

SNAKE: [*offstage, pounding on the door*] Open this door.
WOMAN C: For God's sake.
SNAKE: [*offstage*] Open this door!
WOMAN C: Stop. Stop.
SNAKE: [*offstage*] I'll break this door down if I have to!
WOMAN C: I can't bear it.
SNAKE: [*offstage*] Open up! I'll get the coppers!

    WOMAN C *flings open the door.*

WOMAN C: *Just go away!*

    SNAKE *pushes past her into the room.*

SNAKE: Where's Auntie Eileen? Who are you? Where is she?

WOMAN C: [*sobbing*] Do you want money? Sorry. He only left me fifty dollars. Services rendered. And a note.

SNAKE: Who are you?

WOMAN C: Who am I?

SNAKE: I thought something was up. The houses have all been painted.

WOMAN C: Colin. Colin.

SNAKE: Please tell me.

WOMAN C: What? Have you got a cigarette?

SNAKE: Umm. Here.

WOMAN C: Thank you. [*She sits.*] Much better. I feel…

    Silence.

SNAKE: What's happened?

WOMAN C: He's gone. Seven months. A record for me. But he's gone. No. I'm gone. A perfect find. Good brain, good job, taste, wit, sense of fun, interest in the good things, such as they are. A mother. And a body builder called Manfred. The mother provided the money for this. Deceased estate. Real bargain. You like the colours? The body builder provided late nights and the odd mysterious bruise. Somewhere, late at night, some demands were made. I suspect an ultimatum. I have to go. I box him in. I imprison him. I hang around his neck. Like a dead whatever. So here's fifty dollars to find somewhere else. And a note.

SNAKE: Dead?

WOMAN C: I'm to be gone when he gets home tonight.

SNAKE: No one told us.

WOMAN C: Oh, I'll be gone.

SNAKE: She didn't die in a hospital?

WOMAN C: [*leaning her head on* SNAKE*'s shoulder*] I don't mind pain. I can't bear cruelty.

SNAKE: He doesn't know. They've gone to the shops. A party.

WOMAN C: Oh, I'll be gone.

DEAN: [*offstage*] And it's Deano with the ball forging ahead, making a break, yes, he's sidestepped a nasty tackle there—oh, and he's charging through there—yes, yes—what a player! He's going for—yes, yes—he's through for a try!

DEAN *enters.*

And the crowd goes wild. I couldn't wait. Here I am. Where is she?
SNAKE: Dean—
DEAN: Where is she?
SNAKE: Look—
DEAN: What's up?
SNAKE: Things have changed.
DEAN: You're crying.
SNAKE: I'm not.
DEAN: Auntie Eileen?
SNAKE: Let's go for a drive.
DEAN: *Auntie Eileen!*
SNAKE: Let's. Come on.
DEAN: No. Where is she?
SNAKE: She's… she's…
DEAN: What?
SNAKE: She's dead.

ASPRO *and* DONALD *enter.*

ASPRO: We got Cheezels and Coke.
WOMAN C: And it is not a cry for help.
ASPRO: Are we in the wrong house?
SNAKE: No, we're not.
WOMAN C: A stranger in my own home.
ASPRO: This isn't your home.
SNAKE: Shut up.
ASPRO: It's Auntie Eileen's.
SNAKE: Aspro.
ASPRO: Well, it is.
SNAKE: Do you want a punch in the face or what?
ASPRO: [*to* WOMAN C] Can I have a sip of your drink? Thirsty. Thanks.
SNAKE: Dean, she's dead. There's nothing we can do. We should go.
ASPRO: Who's dead?
SNAKE: No one.
ASPRO: Who's dead?
SNAKE: Dean?
ASPRO: You said she's dead.
WOMAN C: Dead.

ASPRO: Auntie Eileen's dead.
SNAKE: Yes, yes. She's dead. We have to go. Please.
WOMAN C: I'll make some—coffee. Drink? If you'd like to go into… Let's eat him out of house…
ASPRO: Get fucked.
WOMAN C: Exactly.
ASPRO: *Get fucked!*
SNAKE: The Other Thing.
ASPRO: *Get fucked! Get fucked!*
SNAKE: Dean, do something.

> ASPRO *screams and leaps wildly about, opening the door, screaming into the street.* DONALD *and* SNAKE *struggle with him.*
>
> *The* WOMAN *takes some records and scratches them with her fingernails, throwing them around the room.*
>
> *During the confusion* DEAN *takes the woman's pills and pockets them.*
>
> *Finally* ASPRO *subsides.* SNAKE *sits on him, panting.* DONALD *turns off the tape.*
>
> *Silence.*

Dean, please take Aspro to the car. [*To the* WOMAN] He's our brother. He's not well.
WOMAN C: Who is?
SNAKE: I'm very sorry. Can we help clean up?
WOMAN C: No, no. Here. Take the record player. It would give me the—take it. And the television. Great satisfaction. They're yours. Go on. He was building a comprehensive record collection. And a film library. Western civilisation under one roof. He has seven different *Toscas*. Take these. *The Ring*. He was making us save for a trip to Bayreuth. *The Ring*… take it. It's all he… Can I show you… photo…? I found it in a jacket… when the worm first began to turn. 'To Colin, from Manfred with the deepest rearguard.' Why is stupidity so attractive? It was taken at some party. [*Showing* DEAN] I assume that's Manfred, the one dressed as an SS officer. You take it—as a memorial. I… pills… have you seen a bottle? Here—oh. I'll carry the speakers to your car. Can you give me a lift somewhere?
DEAN: No worries.

> *They all go out.*

SCENE SIX

A small flat identical to that in Scene Four, empty.
WOMAN B *comes in, followed by* DEAN.

WOMAN B: This is it. This comprises your entire flat. Higher up, of course, they get bigger, they're actually apartments. The largest is owned by a chap on TV. I can never remember his name, but the face—the face. When I first saw him I thought, 'Now I remember you,' and sure enough it was him. In there, that's your kitchenette.

She follows DEAN *into the kitchen.*

Stove, fridge, cupboard.

They come out.

Shower unit in there. Compact. The venetians are included. View? Yes, there is one. Come here. You really need a chair, but open it up.

They lean out.

See there, between the kiddies' bike factory and the wogs on the corner. That's a bit of the bay, that grey bit, past the smoke stacks. See it? Let me guide your head. Just look straight ahead? See it? Yes, I won't try to hide the fact. I'm worried. Can you pay? You're only a kid. There's no trouble, is there? What about your mother?

He lowers his head.

Ohhh. Just a kid. You're not hiding? Your father's not conducting a heart-breaking search? Just a kid. A very mature kid.

DEAN *signals out the window.*

What do you go in for?
DEAN: Self employed.
WOMAN B: I trust you. Just a kid. There's the keys. Laundry. Letterbox.
DEAN: I'm very grateful.
WOMAN B: I needn't say this, I know, but try and take a bit of pride in the corridors. We've got a couple of wogs come in twice a week and wave a greasy rag about but you'd be amazed how a bit of pride keeps things under control. You'll want to settle in. You'll be amazed what you can fit in here. Nice bookcase, nest of tables, aquarium. And of course your bed.

SNAKE *enters.*

SNAKE: Shit, where's the revolving restaurant?

WOMAN B: We have one hundred and sixty units in the block.

During the following speech DONALD *and* ASPRO *struggle in with the TV, sound equipment and records.*

I believe it's the largest in the Southern Hemisphere. Not counting Housing Commission, of course. There was a lot of opposition to it, of course. Some people'd rather live in tumbledown old shacks or huts like the Abos. Oh, I know it's fashionable to stick up for them, but anyone who'd let kiddies grow up in filth like that isn't worth the trouble. No, against all opposition this place was built. No help from the unions, no help from the locals. The Council actually rushed through a special bylaw to allow it to be built. The Mayor and his wife live on the top floor. I've been up there once. Sweeping views. She's the Chairman of the Residents' Committee. You've got to own before you can be on that. Like everything else. Now: bond. One month's rent in advance, of course.

Silence.

Well, a fortnight, then. I'm not a hard woman.

Silence. They look at DONALD. *He hands over some money.*

Friends are a wonderful thing. Now I trust you. See that trust isn't betrayed.

She goes.

SNAKE: Isn't this tasteful?
DEAN: You don't like it?
SNAKE: Are you sure it's not too spacious?
DEAN: It's the best we can get. We've got no money.
SNAKE: We might have some if some people didn't whinge all the time.
DEAN: I do not whinge.
ASPRO: Ha ha.
DEAN: I suppose you'd rather be in a motel?
DONALD: With a pool on the roof.
DEAN: With a pool on the roof.
ASPRO: It's all right.
SNAKE: Shut up.
DONALD: And a charcoal grill bar.
DEAN: And a coffee shop.

ASPRO: It's a nice flat.
SNAKE: I said shut up.
ASPRO: It's got a window.
SNAKE: Sometimes I wish we'd left you under that bus.
ASPRO: I'm your brother.
SNAKE: I know that.
ASPRO: Well, good.
SNAKE: *How could I forget?!*
ASPRO: *Don't yell!*
SNAKE: *I feel like yelling!*
ASPRO: *Well, me too! It's my problem!*
SNAKE: And now I have this to come home to.
DEAN: I've had to do all the crawling while youse just sat in the car and waited to put your feet up. We're just lucky she was a soft touch. Is that all I'm good for, soft-touching old scags? I get that depressed. Families.
SNAKE: We're supposed to be at the Department in half an hour. I'm getting changed.
ASPRO: I'm not going there ever again. It's torture.
SNAKE: It's too hot to argue with you.

She gets changed.

ASPRO: It's not fair.
SNAKE: Do you want to drive us all crazy or what?
ASPRO: You hate me. That's it, you hate me. That's why you drag me around all those offices. They say, 'No, you've come to the wrong place, Park Street, eighteenth floor'. We walk there. You know that's difficult for me in my condition. We get there. The girl says, 'No, you're in the wrong place. Why did they send you here? Clarence Street, third floor.' We walk there, all the way, in the boiling heat in the middle of the day. We get there. The girl says, 'No, this is the Occupational Section. Liverpool Street, ninth floor.' We walk there. When we get there it's lunchtime. The girl we have to see isn't there. By now I can hardly stand up. We have to wait. We have to take this ticket from this stupid machine and wait for our number to come up. We sit and sit and sit and it's hot and everyone's smelly and sweaty from walking the same streets all the time. We sit and sit and sit and listen to the *Sound of Music* 'Bossa Nova'. There's some smart-arse wants them to see him first 'cause he's really important

'cause he's been there before and someone told him he wouldn't have to wait. But you always have to wait when somebody owes you something. We sit there. We sit and sit. All these cripples and fuckwits like that Irishman from Caringbah. I felt sorry for him, but, he couldn't stop chucking for months. Nothing of him. You're lucky I didn't ask him home with us. Then you'd have been sorry. *At last* the girl comes back from lunch and the numbers start rolling. The girl puts her lippy on behind the counter where everyone can see her, just so we all know how important she is and how we're all in the palm of her hand. You have to wait and wait and wait. Your number gets closer and closer and it gets hotter and hotter. Then, *oh, boy!* Someone's given up in despair so your number's even closer. *Then. At last.* It's your turn. You go over to the counter. She's bored and hot. Goes 'tsk-tsk-tsk'. Rolls her eyes. At the desk behind the counter another girl. Hot. Bored. Rolls her eyes. Sweat in her mo. Rolls her eyes. Some poor sick bugger pours his heart out over the phone. Begging. Pleading for scraps. She's important too. Works in an office. Has a desk and phone. Goes home in the train reading *Cosmo*. Has tea with mum and dad. Complains about all the awful people she sees all day. Boyfriend Greg. Works in the Valuer-General's. Comes over. Watch *Prisoner*. He works his finger up her crack.

SNAKE: Aspro, shut up!

DEAN, *now shirtless, stands at the window in the sun.*

ASPRO: Oh, I know it all. It's all true. They don't care what they say in front of me. I'm too sick to worry about. They talk away. I listen. She asks questions. Fills in the form. Rolls her eyes. Puts her hair behind her ear like this. It keeps falling over her face. She keeps putting it behind her ear 'cause it makes her feel important and busy. She says, 'Have you lodged a previous claim?', and I say, 'Yes', and start to explain. She grinds teeth, rolls eyes. Looks at the girl at the desk. Says, 'Well, it's being attended to,' and I say I can't wait any more. I'm sick. I'm sick. I'm getting sicker and sicker.

DONALD: Sit down. Do you want a drink?

ASPRO: You, you touch me, you little fairy. I'll smash your face in.

SNAKE: Look, leave him alone. Be quiet, Aspro.

DONALD: Would you like me to come with you?

SNAKE: We'll manage.

DEAN: You can go.
ASPRO: No, he can't.
DONALD: I think I'll stay.
DEAN: Go. I'm fine.
DONALD: I could cook something.
ASPRO: I won't eat any.
SNAKE: Shut up.

 SNAKE and ASPRO go. Silence.

DONALD: Don't get burnt. That sun's really strong. Want to hear a record? We could listen to *The Ring*. It's about the end of the world and lasts three weeks. I'm sorry about your auntie. We could go for a swim. They have beaches here where you don't have to wear trunks or anything. Just lie in the sun. In the raw. Lie on the sand. Or climb up on to some rocks away from the other people.
DEAN: [*standing in front of the TV*] What's on?
DONALD: Some movie.
DEAN: What are they doing?
DONALD: Staring at each other.
DEAN: Look at her nose.
DONALD: I think she's telling him he has to go.
DEAN: The arse, eh?
DONALD: 'We'll always be friends.'
DEAN: 'Yeah, but your tits will always be too small.'
DONALD: 'I'll always love you.'
DEAN: 'Love sucks.'
DONALD: 'So do you.'

 He laughs.

DEAN: 'That's why my breath stinks. A-ha.'

 They both laugh.

DONALD: [*laughing*] 'I thought it was my cooking.'
DEAN: Take your hand off my leg.
DONALD: I won't be scared this time.
DEAN: Won't you?
DONALD: No. Can I kiss you again?
DEAN: Can you kiss me?
DONALD: Are you sick of me?
DEAN: Can you kiss me?

DONALD: Tell me what you think of me now? Have you got a word?
DEAN: A word for you?
DONALD: Am I still a brother?

> *Silence.*

I'll do anything you want.

> DEAN *pushes him away and goes into the kitchen. Silence.* DEAN *returns with a drink.*

So what would you like me to cook? What would you like? I'm no great chef. Don't be too outrageous.

> DEAN *watches a piece of paper slide under the door. He suddenly opens the door and drags* DESIREE *in.*

DESIREE: Let go.
DEAN: What's this?
DESIREE: Let go of my arm.
DEAN: What were you doing?
DESIREE: Let go of me, will you?
DEAN: [*reading*] 'Dear Neighbour, I'd just like a few minutes of your precious time to tell you of God's wonderful message.' What's your name?
DESIREE: Let go.
DEAN: What's your name?
DESIREE: Let go of my arm.
DEAN: Okay. What's your name?
DESIREE: Dezray.
DEAN: What?
DESIREE: Dezray.
DEAN: Can't hear you.
DESIREE: *Dez. Ray.*
DEAN: Great name.
DESIREE: It was a film my mother liked. I'd rather be called Ruth.
DEAN: You live in this place?
DESIREE: Downstairs.
DONALD: I'm going now.
DEAN: Sit down.
DESIREE: I have to go too.
DONALD: I'm going shopping now.
DEAN: Go on, sit down.

DESIREE: No. I'll stand here. For a second.
DEAN: Who wrote this?
DESIREE: My father.
DONALD: No special requests, then?

  DONALD *exits*.

DESIREE: I have to go now.
DEAN: You're very skinny.
DESIREE: Compared to what?
DEAN: So, you're just the postie.
DESIREE: I am not. I have my own work.
DEAN: Who do you work for?
DESIREE: I don't have to stand here talking to you.
DEAN: See ya.
DESIREE: My father's the Australasian Distribution Manager for The International Church of the Lord.
DEAN: What's that?
DESIREE: You don't care.
DEAN: I want to know.
DESIREE: It's no joke.
DEAN: Who's laughing?
DESIREE: I don't have time for this.
DEAN: Then why are you doing it?
DESIREE: I have to make the effort. But people don't care. They're not interested. They don't want to hear. They think religion's just some pretty idiot singing, 'Michael, Row the Boat Ashore'. They can't feel it coming. Or they can and pretend not to.
DEAN: What?
DESIREE: 'But the day of the Lord will come as a thief in the night in which the heavens shall pass away with a great noise and the elements will melt with a fervent heat, the earth also and the works that are therein shall be burnt up.'
DEAN: What?
DESIREE: Atomic war.
DEAN: When?
DESIREE: We don't know the exact date. But it's coming.
DEAN: How do you know?
DESIREE: It's in the Bible.
DEAN: My name's Dean.

DESIREE: What do you want?
DEAN: I want to know more. Come for a walk. We could go for a swim.
DESIREE: No way.
DEAN: Don't you look after yourself? If you don't mind me saying, you have a slight odour problem.
DESIREE: What's it to you?
DEAN: Doesn't your old man look after you?
DESIREE: He's too busy. He doesn't have time for that.
DEAN: Relax.
DESIREE: No.
DEAN: You could have a shower here. I'll lend you a towel.
DESIREE: You don't impress me. I'm going.
DEAN: Don't you touch that door.
DESIREE: Why not?
DEAN: I said so.
DESIREE: And who are you?
DEAN: Don't touch that door.
DESIREE: Have a nice day.
DEAN: I want to know more about this war.
DESIREE: Read the papers.
DEAN: Tell me.

Pause.

DESIREE: The International Church of the Lord was founded in nineteen twenty-seven. By Doctor Dwayne B. Patterson. He had a revelation about the meaning of the Bible while reading the Book of Ezekiel. Chapter seven, verse twenty-five: 'Destruction cometh; and they shall seek peace, and there shall be none.' Then his Bible fell open on the last page of the Old Testament and he read: 'For behold, the day cometh, that shall burn as an oven; and all the proud, yea, and all that do wickedness, shall be stubble; and the day cometh shall burn them up, saith the Lord of Hosts, that it shall neither leave them root or branch.' We follow Jesus' command to spread this good news throughout the world. If you're really interested you can subscribe to God's Survival Kit.
DEAN: I'll do it. What is it?
DESIREE: It tells you everything about life. It's the only way to survive what's coming. They're really incredible. They come from America in these big cartons. I don't suppose you've ever been to America?

DEAN: No.

DESIREE: Me neither. I'd like to go. It must be incredible. I'd like to see it before Armageddon. But I'll never be able to afford it. I'll have to wait till after. The President supports us. We've got this photostat of a letter he wrote to Dr Patterson thanking him for his best wishes.

DEAN: How'd you get that nasty bruise?

DESIREE: I fell.

DEAN: On your face?

DESIREE: I tripped.

DEAN: Where's your mother?

DESIREE: Gone. She was no good.

DEAN: And your father is?

DESIREE: He's...

DEAN: Tell us.

DESIREE: He's not a hundred per cent committed. He's belonged to lots of different things since he lost his job. He used to be a security guard. They found out he was a member of this anti-migrant group and made fun of him. He bashed one of them up and got the sack. But when he joined The International Church of the Lord I thought he'd finally found it. I mean there's actual living proof in the Bible of the Second World War, the San Francisco earthquake, everything. Even Australia's mentioned. And you can feel it coming, can't you? Just read the papers. Or look at TV. You can feel the end coming. I can't wait. But Dad...

DEAN: You hate him?

DESIREE: No, not really, He's weak. He's got the answers but he doesn't stick to them. I've never looked back since we joined The International Church of the Lord, but he wavers all the time. He thinks about my mother, I'm sure. Once you accept the Gospel you don't ever have to worry about things, be uncertain. The day our first Kit arrived from America I stopped feeling I had to work everything out for myself. There was this incredible silence in my head. All I have to do now is wait. Sometimes I wake up at night and there's a jet taking off and there's this loud roaring noise. Before I realise what it is I think, '*Now!* It's happening *now!*' I wait for the blinding flash of light, that's the first thing. I race out of bed and get Dad and the shotgun.

DEAN: Shotgun?

DESIREE: When you go down into the shelter you have to take a shotgun with you to fight off the others who want to get in with you. It's in the Kit. I race around getting my things and heading for the door. You have to beat the fireball. Then I realise what it is. I go back to bed. But I can't go back to sleep.

Silence.

Would you like a Kit?
DEAN: Kit?
DESIREE: God's Survival Kit.
DEAN: Yes. I want to know everything.
DESIREE: About God's Wonderful Kingdom to Come?
DEAN: About you.
DESIREE: They cost fifty dollars for the basic Kit and fifteen dollars for a bi-monthly update.
DEAN: Oh. Sorry, I…
DESIREE: Oh. What about a free introductory demonstration?
DEAN: Fantastic.
DESIREE: I'll send Dad up, then.
DEAN: No. I want you.
DESIREE: I can't. I'm not Elect. I'm a girl.
DEAN: I want you. Save me.
DESIREE: It's not allowed.
DEAN: Come up tonight.
DESIREE: I'll say I'm just delivering one for a free trial and that he's to go up later.
DEAN: Unreal.
DESIREE: Let me give you some advice. This building is outside ground zero, that's the area wiped out in the initial blast. All you need to do is head for the basement. It's deep and the walls are thick.
DEAN: Let me give you a few dollars. Buy some shampoo and stuff.
DESIREE: No. I have to go.
DEAN: Tonight.

She goes.

SCENE SEVEN

The Department. A row of seats.

WOMAN D *sits at one end. She stares to her right, then her left.* SNAKE *comes in reading a form.*

SNAKE: Aspro? Aspro?

> *She goes out.* WOMAN D *stares to her right, then her left.* SNAKE *returns.*

'Scuse me. 'Scuse me.

> ASPRO *comes in.*

Where were you?
ASPRO: Dunny.
SNAKE: I told you not to leave that chair. Didn't I? Didn't I?
ASPRO: Yes.
SNAKE: Well, you did.
ASPRO: Yes.
SNAKE: I told you not to.

> *She slaps him.*

Now sit down. Sit down.
ASPRO: I had to go.
SNAKE: I told you not to move.
ASPRO: I'd have done it here.
SNAKE: I don't care. I told you not to move. I wasn't long. You knew I'd be straight back. I wasn't long. You wandered off.
ASPRO: I went to the toilet.
SNAKE: I didn't know that.
ASPRO: I wasn't wandering. I knew where I was going all the time.
SNAKE: I don't care.
ASPRO: To the toilet. I'm pretty sick.

> *Pause.*

SNAKE: Help me fill in this form.
ASPRO: That's wandering, is it?
SNAKE: I don't know.
ASPRO: Is it?
SNAKE: Shut up.

> *Pause.*

ASPRO: I'm hot.
SNAKE: Take your jumper off, stupid.
ASPRO: Nup.
SNAKE: I haven't got a pen.
ASPRO: Ha ha.

SNAKE: Have you got one?
ASPRO: Me?
SNAKE: [*to the* WOMAN] 'Scuse me. 'Scuse me. Have you got a biro? A pen?
ASPRO: Is she looking for someone?
SNAKE: I don't know.
ASPRO: Have you...
SNAKE: Shhh.
ASPRO: ... lost someone?
SNAKE: Shut up.
ASPRO: It's all right.
SNAKE: I'll go and get a pen. Now you stay there. Hear me?
ASPRO: Yes.
SNAKE: Right there.
ASPRO: I'll write you a note if I go away.
SNAKE: Don't you.

> SNAKE *goes out.*

ASPRO: 'Dear Snake, have gone to the bog. Don't worry. Your loving brother, Aspro.'

> *Silence.*

WOMAN D: What they need are a few partitions. [*Pause.*] Across there. And there. And there.

> *Pause.*

ASPRO: Yeah? I'm pretty crook. Are you?
WOMAN D: I'd get him to draw up the plans but he's a bit hard pushed. He could knock them up a noticeboard in no time. They could put their posters on them. In the one place instead of here, there and everywhere.

> SNAKE *comes in.*

SNAKE: Now.
ASPRO: I'm still here.
SNAKE: I know that.
ASPRO: Thanks.
SNAKE: Birthday. Right.
ASPRO: My head hurts worse.
SNAKE: Place of birth. Right.

ASPRO: Real bad.
SNAKE: Education. What year did you get to? Oh, yeah. Employment. Right.

    MAN C comes in and sits next to WOMAN D.

MAN C: Give us a cigarette.
WOMAN D: I'm out.
SNAKE: First complaint lodged. Where's that list?
MAN C: Out?
SNAKE: In my bag.
ASPRO: Bet you've lost it.
SNAKE: Shut up.
MAN C: Arsehole.

    He pushes the WOMAN off the chair.

WOMAN D: You had the packet.
ASPRO: Is she all right?
SNAKE: Shhh. Pay attention. Hold the form.
ASPRO: Didn't you bring the details?
SNAKE: Yes, they're in here somewhere.
MAN C: Cigarette. Jesus.
WOMAN D: I'll get some.
MAN C: Sit down.

    He pulls her back onto the chair.

WOMAN D: There's a machine.
MAN C: No, thanks.
SNAKE: Here it is. Right. Nature of complaint. Honestly. Right. Place of incident. Right.
MAN C: You are so ugly.

    He twists the WOMAN's arm.

  Ugly. Yell. Go on. Yell.

    The WOMAN shakes her head.

  Yell. Cry out. Go on.

    She shakes her head again.

ASPRO: He's hurting her.
SNAKE: Shhh.
ASPRO: Hey!

SNAKE: Shut up.
ASPRO: Cut it out!
SNAKE: Aspro! Just do this with me. Then we can move on.
ASPRO: Oh boy, where next?
SNAKE: Never mind.
ASPRO: I feel sick.
SNAKE: Doctor's certificates. Nil.
ASPRO: I'll have to go.
SNAKE: Are they far?
ASPRO: Nup.

> The MAN *digs around in the woman's bag, empties it on the floor, takes some money and goes out.*

Do you think they're married?
SNAKE: You're very white.
ASPRO: I'll go. Back in a sec.

> ASPRO *goes out unsteadily. The* WOMAN *collects the contents of her bag from the floor. She sits and cries.* SNAKE *tries to ignore her.* SNAKE *offers the her a handkerchief. The* WOMAN *ignores it.* SNAKE *continues to offer it. The* WOMAN *ignores it.* SNAKE *puts the handkerchief back. She looks at the form and sighs.*

SCENE EIGHT

The flat from Scene Six.
DEAN *is alone watching TV.* DONALD *comes in.*

DONALD: I took so long.
DEAN: Don't apologise.
DONALD: The others not back?
DEAN: What do you reckon?
DONALD: Did you go for a swim?
DEAN: No. You're in the way.
DONALD: Sorry. Have you seen the news?
DEAN: No.
DONALD: I thought there might have been something about the fires. The city's surrounded by fire. The air is full of ash. I got some food. Do you like artichokes? There are fires in the town as well. They start by themselves it's so hot. Spontaneous combustion. All the

streets are blocked off. The city's at a standstill. I got something for you. It's a portable stereo. You can wear it anywhere. On the beach, lie in the sun, listening to your favourite music. I stole it. I went into this hi-fi shop and wandered around for a while. I talked to this young guy about speakers and turntables. I said I'd think about it. I acted being uncertain really well. Picking and choosing. Looking around. After about half an hour I knew the layout of the shop really well. Near the door was a counter with the cash register. Then four aisles running to the back like a supermarket with small equipment and parts and extras. At the back stereo systems all set up in this carpeted area with mood lighting and comfortable chairs. These were about halfway along one of the aisles. The only worry was those mirrors they have so they can see what's going on. I got myself out of range of all of them and it just fell into the groceries. The hardest part was not to rush out straight away. I looked really depressed about not being able to choose and collected all these pamphlets to go home and think about it. I took a deep breath and headed past the front counter. I smiled this really weak smile. 'Isn't it hard to choose when you're so wealthy and there's so much to choose from?' He understood and smiled back. I just wandered along the street for five minutes. I was nearly sick. I never knew your legs really went weak with fear. Do you like it?

DEAN: What's the tape in it?
DONALD: *Fidelio*. Highlights.
DEAN: Unreal.
DONALD: I bought it with the last of my money. I'm penniless.
DEAN: That's a worry.

A knock at the door.

It's open.

DESIREE *drags a carton in.*

Nearly given you up.
DESIREE: I got sidetracked. Enquiries.
DEAN: Have another fall?
DESIREE: On the stairs.
DEAN: Sure?
DESIREE: I fell. I did.
DEAN: Bump your head as well?

He locks the door.

DESIREE: On the door.
DEAN: The door?
DONALD: Should I start cooking now?
DEAN: Forget it. I'll shove them in the kitchen. Drink?

DEAN *exits.*

DONALD: No, thanks.
DESIREE: No, I thought only he—on his own. I'll have to go.
DONALD: No. No, I'll go. It's all right. I think it's time I went.
DESIREE: No, I'll have to go. He said only he'd be here.
DONALD: No. It's a good opportunity. I...
DESIREE: No, you stay.
DONALD: I am tired.
DESIREE: Oh. Oh, well.
DONALD: You may as well stay too.
DESIREE: It's just that he... Dean...
DONALD: Oh, look.
DESIREE: But it's all right. [*To* DEAN, *offstage*] I can't stay too long.
DONALD: I could go for a swim.
DESIREE: No, no, stay. I don't mind.
DONALD: You're sure?
DESIREE: Oh, yes. [*To* DEAN, *offstage*] I can't stay too long, that's all.
DONALD: Or else what?
DESIREE: Nothing.

There is a pounding on the door.

Who's that?
DONALD: That'll be Snake and Aspro.
DESIREE: You know them?

DEAN *re-enters.*

Are you sure it's them?
DEAN: Expecting anyone else?
DESIREE: No, no.
DEAN: [*shouting at the door*] That you?
SNAKE: [*offstage*] Who else?
DESIREE: I got a fright.

DEAN *lets them in.*

SNAKE: Why the fuck's the door locked?
DEAN: Well?
SNAKE: Frightened we'd get robbed?
DEAN: Well?
SNAKE: A well is a hole in the ground.
DEAN: Good day?
SNAKE: I'm tired.
DEAN: I'm not going to beg.
SNAKE: Marvellous.
DEAN: We're having a get-together.
SNAKE: We don't need a get-together.
DEAN: Fuck, you're touchy.
DONALD: How is he?
SNAKE: Pardon?
DONALD: How is he?
SNAKE: Is someone asking after Aspro? I need a chair.

She sits on the carton.

DESIREE: Don't sit on that. It's valuable.
SNAKE: I'm so sorry. What's that smell?
DONALD: [*silently*] Her.
DESIREE: Who are these?
SNAKE: These?
DEAN: My sister Yvonne. And Aspro.
DESIREE: Oh, I don't know about all these people.
SNAKE: Oh, I'm so sorry. Come on, Aspro. We'll find a gutter to lie in.
DESIREE: Oh, no. Stay.
SNAKE: Oh, no. He should lie down anyway.
DEAN: Stay.
DESIREE: Yes… stay.
SNAKE: You're sure it's all right?
DEAN: We're all staying.
SNAKE: Thank you so much. Aspro, your prezzie.
ASPRO: Oh. I nicked these for you. Sorry I yelled at you.

He gives DONALD *a box of chocolates.*

DONALD: Thank you. Are you all right?
ASPRO: Nup. Can I have one?
DONALD: You open them.

ASPRO: You. My hands shake too much.
DESIREE: [*unpacking a slide projector with audio unit*] I'll set this up. I'll have to be quick. Where's the power point? The same as in our place? Yes. I hope I get this right. I've never done this before.
SNAKE: Is she crook or what?
DEAN: Shut up.
SNAKE: Aspro, are you all right?
ASPRO: Head.
SNAKE: Have an aspro.
ASPRO: I'll have two. With a choccie.
DEAN: All right. Did you see them?
SNAKE: Don't worry yourself.
DEAN: What did they say?
SNAKE: Gave us their opinion.
DEAN: And-Did-You-Get-The-Money?
SNAKE: You're incredible.
DEAN: What did I do?
SNAKE: There won't be any money. [*Pause.*] A loophole.
DEAN: Loophole?
SNAKE: A paragraph. This…clause. Nothing.

Silence. Sirens in the distance.

ASPRO: What have we got? 'Coffee Crème. Freshly roasted coffee in a delightful, rich soft crème. They've spelt cream wrong.
DONALD: It's French.
ASPRO: Oh, thanks. 'Apricot Oval. Exotic fon… fond… fond-ont flowing from a smooth chocolate oval. Amorée.'
DONALD: It means love.
DEAN: [*all the while watching* DESIREE] Shucks.
ASPRO: 'A whole hazelnut smothered in hazelnut nougat paste and dipped in luscious chocolate.' God. A whole hazelnut!
DESIREE: We should get started.
SNAKE: Hurray, hurray.
DESIREE: Hope the screen stays up. There. You're going to enjoy this. Everyone does. Ready? Oh, the lights.

DONALD turns them off.

DONALD: Look at the sunset.
DESIREE: You'd better shut the venetians.

DONALD: Hang on. [*He shuts the venetians.*] There.
DESIREE: Right. Ready? Um. I push this for the slides and this for the tape. Ready?
SNAKE: Yes.
DESIREE: Right.

She starts the projector.

VOICE: [*in an American accent*] Why is there so much strife in our world?

Slide: The Berlin Wall.

Why are so many governments so evil?

Slide: A riot.

Where is today's violence heading? To the end of the world as we know it. Where shall the end come from? Gard has told us.

Slide: The Kremlin.

Russian music.

DONALD: That's Tchaikovsky.
VOICE: It is clear in Gard's Word that Russia, or Gog as she is known, will one day soon rise upon against the true Israel and wreak a terrible destruction.

Slide: An atomic mushroom upside down.

DESIREE: Oh, sorry.

They all turn upside down.

VOICE: 'In all your dwelling places the cities shall be laid waste,' says the prophet Ezekiel, 'Few will be saved in this terrible holocaust'.
SNAKE: This is ridiculous.
DEAN: Shhh.

Slide: Post-bomb Hiroshima.

VOICE: The world will be laid waste. When? Soon. Will you survive? Gard can show you how.

Slide: Desert war.

First you can learn to interpret the signs Gard will send us. 'Wars and rumours of wars', said Gard's advance warning system, his own son Jesus Christ.

Slide: A volcanic eruption.

There will be terrible earthquakes. Natural disasters on a vast scale. Thousands upon thousands will perish in catastrophic accidents and catastrophes.

Slide: The UN headquarters building.

So-called peacemakers will lose control. World tempers will grow short. Reason will give way to desperation in international affairs.

Slide: An empty highway.

Shrinking resources.

Slide: A starving child.

Too little food and over-population will force those peoples hostile to the Lord's people—America, Britain and the white English-speaking Commonwealth countries—into open confrontation. Learn to be ready for this exciting event. But you must also learn how to survive.

Slide: Another atomic mushroom.

The survivors will be few. The destruction will be vast, unimaginable.

Slide: A Hiroshima victim.

Those not destroyed in the initial blasts will die of terrible burns, or the dreadful lingering death of radiation sickness. Desperate measures will be needed for the Lord's people to survive.

Slide: A man with a shotgun.

Like the sinners desperate to get into Noah's Ark, men will try to share your safety. You must know how to protect yourself and your loved ones.

Slide: Tanks.

DESIREE *recites with the tape.*

Truly frightful times lie ahead for this world. The handwriting is on the wall.

Slide: A bearded man in book-lined study.

This is Dr Dwayne B. Patterson. I urge you to put your name on our Holy Register. Time is running out. Let us unveil for you the plan for Gard's destruction of the world. Let us prepare you now for the coming horror. Will you perish? Is everlasting agony to be your lot? Reflect. You must decide now.

SNAKE *has turned on Aspro's radio.*

DEAN: Turn that off.
SNAKE: No.
DEAN: I'm listening.
SNAKE: Let's dance.

She turns on the TV.

DEAN: I said turn it off.
SNAKE: Let's have a real get-together.
DEAN: I was listening.
DESIREE: I'll have to go. It's late.
DEAN: You stay there.
DESIREE: No, I'll have to go.
DEAN: You stay there. [*To* SNAKE] Turn that off.
SNAKE: Leave it alone.
DEAN: I'm getting pretty sick and tired.
SNAKE: Leave it, Dean.
DEAN: You're always such a pain in the arse.
SNAKE: I want to dance. *Louder.*

The slides begin to flash through again.

ASPRO: Louder.
SNAKE: Dance.
DESIREE: I'll pick this up later.

DEAN *throws her down.*

DEAN: Stay there and shut up.
ASPRO: [*lurching around*] Louder!
DEAN: [*to* SNAKE] You're lucky I don't beat the shit out of you.
SNAKE: Go on, go on.

DONALD *turns off the noise.*

DEAN: What do you know? Nothing. Nothing.
SNAKE: I know we're broke.
DEAN: Well, you can fix that.
SNAKE: Not this time.
DEAN: It's all you're good at.
SNAKE: Don't touch me.
DEAN: [*dragging her to the door*] Get out there. Go on. Come back with some takeaway when you've finished.
SNAKE: Let go of me.

DONALD: You're hurting her.
DEAN: Get out of it, girlie. Go and get a job as a hairdresser.
DONALD: You'll hurt her.
SNAKE: I can look after myself.
DEAN: Go and find a public toilet and sing opera to a window dresser.
DONALD: Just let go of her.

> *He punches* DEAN.

SNAKE: [*to* DONALD] Don't you hit him. Don't you.
DEAN: [*to* DONALD] Scratch my eyes out. Go on.

> ASPRO *vomits blood.*

ASPRO: Help me.

> *Pause.* MAN B, *Desiree's father, comes in. She follows him meekly out.*

SNAKE: Aspro.
ASPRO: Help me.

> *Pause.*

SNAKE: Just lie down.

> *Pause.*

DONALD: I'll get an ambulance.
SNAKE: No.
DONALD: He'll have to go. Hospital.
SNAKE: Steven? Steven?
ASPRO: Oh, help me.
SNAKE: Hold my arm.
ASPRO: Please don't touch me.
DONALD: We'll have to go now. We'll drive him.
DEAN: Here's the keys.
ASPRO: Oh, help me.

> SNAKE, ASPRO *and* DONALD *exit.* DEAN *collects cigarettes, portable stereo and jacket and goes out.*

SCENE NINE

The flat from Scene Four.

MAN B *sits at the table. There is pounding on the door. Finally he opens the door.* DEAN *enters.*

DEAN: You must be proud of her. Can I see her? I was that impressed. You're not upset with her, are you? If she's upset you in any way, blame me. She here? [*He checks the kitchen, then comes back in.*] Where is she?

> *He looks at the wardrobe. The* MAN *moves to it.* DEAN *beats him there.*

You know what your problem is? In a word, I'd say you were paranoid. Know what that means? Means you worry too much. I don't worry. Not worth it. This place stinks. That's what gave you away. Had a dog once smelt like that.

> *He opens the wardrobe. He pulls out* DESIREE, *bound and beaten. She is tied to a shotgun.* DEAN *undoes the rope.*

Been falling down stairs again? You'll have to learn to be more careful. I have a present for you. Portable stereo, see? These go on you head. Turn it up. Great, eh?

> DEAN *sits her down. She sits, listening.*
>
> DEAN *aims the gun at the* MAN *and pushes him into the kitchen. Beating noises, choking. Noise, then silence.*
>
> DESIREE *sits, stunned, listening. Sirens.*
>
> DEAN *comes in, removes the headset, takes the gun and leads* DESIREE *out.*

Don't look back. Don't look back. Don't look back.

SCENE TEN

Open ground somewhere.

DESIREE *struggles to get up.*

DEAN: Relax.
DESIREE: Let go, let go.
DEAN: I wish you'd relax.
DESIREE: Let go.
DEAN: Look at the sky. Red, eh?
DESIREE: I have to go back.
DEAN: You can't.
DESIREE: I will.

DEAN: Calm down.
DESIREE: Let go.
DEAN: Just relax.
DESIREE: Let go.

   She bites him.

DEAN: Ow. Cunt.

   He goes to hit her.

DESIREE: No, no!
DEAN: I didn't mean—
DESIREE: Let me go.
DEAN: We could go for a swim. Ever been swimming at night?
DESIREE: Help me back.
DEAN: No.
DESIREE: I have to go back.
DEAN: Let's get going, then. Time to go.
DESIREE: I'm not going anywhere with you.
DEAN: Yes you are.
DESIREE: What'll I do now?
DEAN: I'll be like a brother. Let's go. We have the gun. We're ready for anything. We're ready to just go down into the shelter. You'll go first and I'll cover you.
DESIREE: I don't want you. You won't be there.
DEAN: I will.
DESIREE: You won't ever know. You'll be caught out like everyone else. You'll go up in smoke. Or you'll lie in a street, red. A red blister. Red. You'll be sick. Your gums will bleed. That's what happens. Your hair falls out. You'll be sick like you've never been sick. Your skin melts. You'll be so thirsty. You'd kill for a drop of water but your mouth will be melted. Let go.
DEAN: Have a few of these pills.

   He produces the bottle of pills and crams some in her mouth.

DESIREE: No.
DEAN: They'll calm you down.
DESIREE: No. [*She spits them out.*] I'm alone. I don't want you.

   Silence. Sirens.

DEAN: I'll get the car. You stay here. Mind the gun. I'll come back and pick you up. I will.

He goes.

DESIREE: [*shouting after him*] *You'll be left outside! You'll die at the door of the shelter! I'll hear you scratching!*

Silence. She closes her eyes tight.

End. Now.

She opens her eyes.

SCENE ELEVEN

The flat as in Scene Eight.

DONALD *sits listening to the end of* Die Walküre.

SNAKE *comes in and sits. The record ends.*

DONALD: Back? I was listening to *The Valkyrie*. That was the end when she's put to sleep forever. Till a hero comes through the flames to wake her up. Hot. So still you can hear the cockroaches breeding. Want to hear something else?

SNAKE: No.

DONALD: I thought you might like something cheery. *Twilight of the Gods*.

He laughs. Silence. Sirens.

Fire engines. How is he?

She shrugs.

So hot.

SNAKE: Is it?

DONALD: Want a drink?

SNAKE: No.

DONALD: No messages?

SNAKE: He can't speak.

DONALD: Did they say how long he'd be there?

SNAKE: No.

DONALD: Didn't they say anything?

SNAKE: This and that. [*She starts to cry.*] Serious. Critical. [*Stopping herself*] When we came down here for holidays Auntie Eileen'd take us up the pub and we'd sit on the footpath and they'd all come out and talk to Dean and show him their medals and their greyhounds.

Sometimes he'd show them this tattoo he had done as a joke up at Wally Hammond's up the Cross. I didn't want Aspro to go near a hospital. You have no control over your own body. They talk about Russia.

She cries. DONALD *puts his arm around her.* DEAN *comes in.*

DEAN: You on the turn? [*He turns on the TV.*] How about a drink?
SNAKE: I'll get it.
DONALD: No, you—
SNAKE: [*savagely*] I said I'll get it.

SNAKE *goes out.*

DONALD: I'm going.
DEAN: Yeah?
DONALD: Waited till Snake was back. See she was all right.
DEAN: Big of you.

Silence.

DONALD: Well. Goodbye.
DEAN: Ta-ta.
DONALD: Tell Snake…

DONALD *goes.* DEAN *watches TV. Sirens.* SNAKE *re-enters.*

SNAKE: Aspro died at half past ten. Here's your drink.

He takes the drink. She grabs his arm and twists it.

Yell. Go on. Yell. Cry out. Go on.
DEAN: Get out of it.

SNAKE *packs a few things, watching TV as she does so. She takes a case and leaves, turning out the light.*

DEAN *takes out the pills. He takes one, then another. He takes more.*

THE END

GRIFFIN THEATRE COMPANY PRESENTS

The Kid
by Michael Gow

Cast

Donald	**Eamon Farren**
Snake	**Emma Palmer**
Aspro	**Andrew Ryan**
Dean	**Akos Armont**
Desiree	**Yael Stone**
The Women	**Kelly Butler**
The Men	**Mark Pegler**

Production

Director	**Tom Healey**
Designer	**Gabrielle Logan**
Lighting Designer	**Luiz Pampolha**
Composer/ Sound Designer	**Nick Wishart**
Fight Director	**Gavin Robins**
Assistant Director	**Shane Jones**
Production Manager	**Miles Thomas**
Stage Manager	**Belinda Di Lorenzo**

Griffin Theatre Company's season of the *The Kid* opened at the SBW Stables Theatre, Sydney on 19 March 2008.

The Kid was first performed at the Winter Theatre, Fremantle on 25 August 1983.

Cover photo by Olivia Martin-McGuire.

Griffin Theatre Company

The SBW Stables Theatre

Griffin is Australia's leading new writing theatre. It develops, produces and promotes contemporary Australian theatre texts in a way that is fresh, passionate, challenging and entertaining. Griffin is the only professional theatre company in Sydney entirely dedicated to this work.

Griffin is one of the Australian theatre's great engine rooms. The hit films *Lantana* and *The Boys* began life as plays produced by Griffin and playwright Michael Gow launched his career through Griffin with the premiere productions of *Away* – now Australia's most loved contemporary play – and *Europe*. Many other plays premiered by Griffin are produced regularly throughout Australia and internationally. Many actors have begun their professional careers at Griffin, including Cate Blanchett and Jacqueline McKenzie.

Griffin is a place of good beginnings.

Griffin is the resident theatre company at the historic SBW Stables Theatre and is proud to curate the venue on behalf of its owner, the Seaborn, Broughton and Walford Foundation. In 2008, the theatre will host five Griffin season productions as well as five Griffin Stablemates collaborations and other events.

Griffin Theatre Company
13 Craigend Street, Kings Cross NSW 2011
Phone: 9332 1052
Fax: 9331 1524
Email: info@griffintheatre.com.au
Web: www.griffintheatre.com.au

SBW Stables Theatre
10 Nimrod Street, Kings Cross NSW 2011
Bookings: 1300 306 776
or online at
www.griffintheatre.com.au

Michael Gow
Writer

Michael Gow is both a Director and Playwright. He has worked with most of Australia's leading performance companies and a number of overseas theatre organisations. In his current role as Artistic Director of Queensland Theatre Company, he has directed *Who's Afraid of Virginia Woolf?*, *John Gabriel Borkman*, *Private Fears in Public Places*, *Private Lives* (co-production with State Theatre of South Australia), *Away* (co-production with Griffin Theatre), *Oedipus the King*, *The Venetian Twins*, *The Cherry Orchard*, *The Real Inspector Hound*, *Black Comedy*, *Phedra*, *We Were Dancing*, *The Fortunes of Richard Mahony* (co-production with Playbox), *Cooking with Elvis*, *Bag O' Marbles*, *The Tragedy of King Richard III* (collaboration with The Bell Shakespeare Company),*The Tragedy of King Richard the Second*, *Buried Child*, *Dirt*, *Fred*, *Shopping & F$$$ing*, *Mrs Warren's Profession*, *The Skin of Our Teeth* and *XPO – The Human Factor*. Michael has also directed a number of productions with Sydney Theatre Company, where he was Associate Director from 1991 to 1993, Company B, Black Swan Theatre Company, Griffin Theatre Company, State Theatre Company of South Australia, Australian Theatre for Young People, Playbox, Opera Australia, Sydney Festival and Adelaide Festival. Michael's writing credits for stage, screen and radio are extensive. His plays include the multi-award winning play *Away*, *The Kid*, *On Top of The World*, *Europe*, *1841*, *Furious*, *Sweet Phoebe*, *Live Acts on Stage* and *The Fortunes of Richard Mahony*. In 2007 Michael has also directed *The Abduction From the Seraglio* for Opera Australia. His latest play, *Toy Symphony*, premiered with Company B in 2007 and won seven Sydney Theatre Critics awards including Best New Australian Work. Griffin has enjoyed a long association with Michael Gow, having presented five of his plays *Away*, *The Kid*, *Europe*, *Live Acts on Stage* and *Sweet Phoebe* over the last twenty-five years.

Tom Healey
Director

Tom graduated from the VCA acting course in 1989. From 1999-2003 he was Artistic Associate at Playbox. He was the Casting Consultant and Artistic Counsel at the Malthouse Theatre from 2005-7. He has also held the positions of Curator for the Australian National Playwrights' Conference, Artistic Directorate for Hothouse Theatre and Panelist for Arts Victoria. Tom's directing credits include *The Spook* (Malthouse Theatre); Eddie Perfect's two solo shows, *Drink Pepsi Bitch* (Malthouse/Sydney Opera House) and *Angry Eddie*; *The Laramie Project* and *Julius Caesar* (NIDA); *Elegy*, *The Sign of the Seahorse*, *Ancient Enmity*, *Insouciance*, *The Fat Boy and Falling Petals* (Playbox); *Salt Creek Murders* and *Into the Web* (Mainstreet Theatre Company); *The Normal Heart* and *Reckless* (Theatreworks); *Sharon Lily Screwdriver* and *Spumante Romantica* (Napier St Theare); *Metro Street* (Production Company); *A View of Concrete* (Victorian Arts Centre, Wal Cherry Play of the year); *Blind Faith* (The Storeroom); *Hamlet: Explorations* (MTC); *Magnet, Victory Girls* and *The Sax Diaries* (La Mama); *The Imaginary Invalid*, *The Kid* (VCA); *Merrily We Roll Along, Company, Prodigal* and *Working* (Arts Academy); *Fanshen, Top Girls* and *Angels In America pt 1* (National Theatre Drama School). As resident, Lindy Hume's production of *Carmina Burana* (Australian Ballet) and national tour of Robyn Nevin's production of *Summer of the Seventeenth Doll* (MTC). Opera credits include *City Life* (OzOpera, with Lindy Hume), *The Turn of the Screw* and *The Marriage of Figaro* (Canberra School of Music), *Iolantha* and *Viva La Mama* (VCA), *The Opera Project* (Melbourne Conservatorium. This is Tom's first production for Griffin.

Eamon Farren

Eamon graduated from NIDA in 2007. Since graduating his television credits include *All Saints* and *The Sleepover Club*. He has also appeared in the film *The Outsider* and the HBO minseries *The Pacific*. Whilst at NIDA he appeared in *Kiss of the Spiderwoman, Sweet Charity, The Rivals, The Lost Echo, Hamlet* and *The Cherry Orchard*. This is Eamon's first production with Griffin. Eamon is a proud member of the Actor's Equity.

Emma Palmer

Emma is a 2007 graduate of NIDA. Originally a classical dancer, Emma completed a Bachelor of Creative Arts at Melbourne University. Her student credits include *Top Girls, The Incorruptible, The Vagina Monologues* and the Melbourne University Comedy Review, as well as several Melbourne Fringe Festival productions including *People Watching*, an original Australian work at 45 Downstairs. Favourite roles at NIDA include: Katja in *White Russian*; Zillah Katz in *A Bright Room Called Day*; Antonia in *Can't*

Pay, Won't Pay; Elaine in *One Good Beating*; Gertrude in *Hamlet* and Arkadina in *The Seagull*. This is Emma's first production for Griffin. Emma is a proud member of the Actors Equity.

Andrew Ryan

Andrew graduated from QUT in 2006. Since graduating Andrew has appeared in the feature films *Black Balloon* and *All My Friends are Leaving Brisbane* and the short film *A Match of Priorities*. His television credits include *Double the Fist* and *All Saints*. Whilst at QUT, Andrew appeared in *Once in a Lifetime, Lion in the Street, Our Country's Good, Terrain, Terrain, Terrain, Twelfth Night* and *Camille*. This is Andrew's first production for Griffin. Andrew is a proud member of the Actors Equity.

Akos Armont

Akos graduated from NIDA in 2007. Since graduating he has appeared in the HBO miniseries *The Pacific*. Whilst at NIDA he appeared in *Kiss of the Spiderwoman, Sweet Charity, The Rivals, Hamlet* and *The Seagull*. This is Akos' first production with Griffin. He is a member of the Actors Equity.

Yael Stone

Yael graduated from NIDA in 2006. Her film and television credits include *West, Me Myself I, All Saints* and *The Farm*. Whilst at NIDA, Yael appeared in *Yours Sincerely, The Laramie Project, The Attic, Afterplay, Cymbeline* and *the London Cuckolds*. This is Yael's first production with Griffin. She is a member of the Actors Equity.

Kelly Butler

Kelly graduated from NIDA in 1993. She also has a Diploma In Acting from 'The School Of Arts', University Of Queensland. Her television credits include *Murder in The Outback, All Saints, Love My Way Seasons 1, 2* and *3, McLeod's Daughters, To Catch a Killer, The Alice, Small Claims, Farscape 4, CNNNN/The Chaser, The Rubicon, The Farm, Water Rats, Home and Away, Murder Call* and *Passion: The Gun in History*. Kelly's film credits include *The Last Chip, Twists of Fate, The Matrix II & III, The Crop* and *Straight To You* and the short films *Fued, Arkadia, Going Out, Grey* and *fOUR*. She has performed many Radio Plays for ABC Radio National including Christina in *Embers and*

The Detective in The Monkeys Mask. Her extensive theatre credits include *Corporate Vibes, Third World Blues, The John Wayne Principle, Dead White Males* and *Sydney Stories* (Sydney Theatre Company); *Blue Murder* (Belvoir St Theatre); *Later then Spring* (Marian St Theatre); *Good Works* (Q Theatre Company); *Milo* (Theatre South); *Phaedra* (TN Theatre Company); and *Soldier Boy* (Canute Productions Pty Ltd). This is Kelly's second production for Griffin having also performed in *Passion*. She is a member of the Actors Equity.

Mark Pegler

Mark graduated from NIDA in 1984. Mark's television credits include *Home and Away, All Saints, Blue Heelers, Stingers, Round the Twist IV, Dogwoman 2, The Last of the Ryans, Phoneix II, A Country Practice, Flying Doctors* and *Vietnam*. Mark's theatre credits include: *Blithe Spirit, The Duchess of Malfi, The Tempest, Private Lives, Julius Caesar, My Father's Father* (MTC); *Festen, Embers, The White Devil, Private Lives, Blithe Spirit, A Midsummer Night's Dream, All My Sons, Romeo and Juliet, Dance of Death* (STC); *Entertaining Mr Sloane*, (STCSA); *Slow Love,* (Chambermade Opera); *King Lear* and *Wolf* (Playbox); *Capricornia* (Company B); *Merchant of Venice* (Bell Shakespeare); *Three Sisters* (Hildegarde); *Titus, The Normal Heart* (Theatreworks); *Victory Girl, The Brand New Ford* (La Mama); *Noises Off* (Comedy Theatre, Melbourne); *Bombay to Beijing by Bicycle* (Castlemaine Festival); *Front* (Melbourne Workers Theatre); *The Gap* (Chameleon); *That Eye the Sky* (Burning House); *Nuti & Kikimora* (Meryl Tankard's Australian Dance Theatre); *Little Malcolm and his Struggle Against the Eunuchs* (O'Punsky's); *Breaking the Silence, Otherwise Engaged* (Marian Street) and *The Golden Age, Tartuffe* and *The Winters Tale* (Nimrod). This is Mark's first Griffin production. He is a member of the Actors Equity.

Gabrielle Logan
Designer

Gabrielle graduated from NIDA in 2007. Prior to finishing the design course at NIDA, Gabrielle had extensive training in both fashion and graphic design. During 2003 and 2004 she involved herself in community based amateur theatre and worked with both the Newcastle Repertory Theatre and the Young Peoples Theatre Company in the Hunter Valley. In 2004 she undertook a period of work experience with Opera Australia, where she assisted on the production Baroque Masterworks. Post graduation Gabrielle has designed for NIDA's Open Program and assisted on the Pinchgut Opera production *Juditha Triumphans*. Whilst at NIDA Gabrielle worked on: *Private Life of a Master Race, Julius Caesar, Games Of Love and Chance, A Body Of Water* and *Footprints*. This is Gabrielle's first production for Griffin.

Luiz Pampolha
Lighting Designer

Luiz' lighting credits include: *Love-Lies-Bleeding* (STC); *Hitler's Daughter, The Prospectors* (Monkey Baa); *Back In Your Box, Boy Overboard, Three Little Fears, This Territory* (atyp); *Somewhere, Weather* (Q); *Arabian Night* (NIDA); *Half & Half, Blasted, A Number, 7 Blowjobs, Now That Communism Is Dead My Life Feels Empty, Love* (B-Sharp); *Cloud 9, The Illusion, The Mystery of Irma Vep, The Drowned World, Bangers & Mash, The No Chance In Hell Hotel, Bone* (Darlinghurst Theatre Company); *Singing The Lonely Heart, The Man Who* (New Theatre); *A Couple of Blaguards* (AMcK); *CODA, danceTank* (Sydney Opera House); and *Capture the Flag, This Blasted Earth, Cu*t Pi, Thrall, Little Boy, Harry's Christmas, Mother Teresa Is Dead, Tragedy: a tragedy, The Suitors, Constance Drinkwater* (TRS). Luiz, a Sydney Theatre Critics Award Nominee in 2006, is a NIDA graduate and has also designed and co-designed productions for the Edinburgh Fringe, Adelaide Fringe, Belfast and Melbourne International Arts Festivals. This is Luiz's third production for Griffin after designing the lighting for *The Nightwatchman* and *The Story of the Miracles at Cookie's Table*.

Nick Wishart
Sound Designer

Electronic Musician and chronic Circuit Bender, Nick Wishart composes soundtracks for theatre and creates unique instruments that form the basis of Toydeath (an all toy band). Nick has composed soundtracks for many of Australia's premier theatre companies including Sydney Theatre Co, Urban Theatre Projects, Circus Monoxide, ERTH, Salamanca Theatre Company, and Jigsaw Theatre Company. Nick is also a composer and collaborator on CeLL a MIDI controlled pneumatic orchestra. This is Nick's second production for Griffin after creating the sound design for *October*.

Shane Jones
Assistant Director

Shane is a 2006 NIDA Directing Program graduate and has also completed a BA in Theatre Studies at Queensland University of Technology. In 2007 he travelled to New York to train with Anne Bogart and the Saratoga International Theatre Institute. Recent directing credits include: *Hong Kong: Fa Hoi Fu Kwai* (Zen Zen Zo Physical Theatre), *The Caretaker* (Vena Cava); *Mountain Language, New World Order, The Dumb Waiter, The Rain, The Refuge, Terror, Disorientation and Fear* (devised) and *The Rape of Innocence* (devised) at NIDA. Previous directing credits include: Steven Berkoff's *Agamemnon* for QUT; *Harry's Christmas* for Central Queensland University, *The Oracle* for osmosis dance-theatre at The Brisbane Powerhouse, the documentary *FIVE: Five Days, Five Mates, $500* for Centenary of Federation Queensland, songs for La Boite's New Boards Festival. In 2008 Shane will direct the Queensland premiere of *Motortown* in July at the Metro Arts in Brisbane and the Australian premiere of *The Unearthed Remains of Victor Lodge* in November at the Brisbane Powerhouse. This is Shane's first production with Griffin.

Miles Thomas

In 2006 Miles was production coordinator for the Paris Opera Ballet's Sydney tour and toured to Melbourne Comedy festival as producer and Lighting Designer for *Strangelove: The Musical*. Previously he has worked in a wide range of production roles for shows including *Woomera* and *Woyeck* at the Old Fitzroy Hotel Theatre and *Into the Woods* (SUDS). Over the past few years he has also worked as a Lighting Technician and Head Electrician for Sydney Theatre Company, The Seymour Centre and The Capitol Theatre. First joining Griffin in their 2007 season, Miles has production managed *The Nightwatchman, October, The Story of the Miracles at Cookie's Table, King Tide, China* and *Impractical Jokes*.

Belinda di Lorenzo
Stage Manager

Belinda is a 2007 Production graduate from NIDA and also studied at University of Western Sydney in a Bachelor of Performance Theory and Practice (Theatremaking). Belinda's credits include creating a collaboration of work for Penrith Youth Festival 2004; Assistant stage manager, DasShoku HORA at the Sydney Opera House in 2007; and most recently Stage Managed OnStage at Seymour Centre Sydney in 2008. Whilst at NIDA, Belinda's credits include *Private Life of the Master Race* (Sound Designer); *Three Sisters*, (Stage Manager /Sound Designer); *Closer*, (Deputy Stage Manager); and *Directors Project 2005* (Production Coordinator). Her secondment credits include Australia Day 2007, Operations and Logistics intern; Sydney Opera House Producers Unit, Assistant to producing team; Company the musical, Assistant to stage management; CarriageWorks; Assistant to executive producer. This is Belinda's first show with Griffin.

Go to the theatre more often...

Interesting Fact #1

Did you know people carry around different running tabs in their heads?

You have, for example, an "entertainment account." Losing a theatre ticket and replacing it costs your entertainment account $100 instead of the planned $50. Lost cash, however, is charged to another account - which is why most people would replace a theatre ticket even after they lost some cash but not if they lost a ticket.

The $50 theatre ticket should be equal to the $50 cash, but human beings don't think this way, which is why economic models of human behaviour often turn out to be wrong.

Thinking like an accountant can free you up to enjoy all that life has to offer

**For expert financial advice
Tel: 1300 753 222**

www.pkf.com.au

right size. right people. right answers.®

PKF

Chartered Accountants
& Business Advisers

Griffin Theatre Company

Patron Dr Rodney Seaborn AO, OBE
Board Hilary Bell, Michael Bradley (Chair), Dianne Davis (Deputy Chair), Lisa Lewin (Treasurer), Simon Burke, Tina Bursill, Victoria Doidge, Nick Marchand, Kate O'Brien, Stuart Thomas

Artistic Director Nick Marchand
General Manager Nathan Bennett
Special Projects Manager Rosie Fisher
Administrator Belinda Kelly
Finance Manager Will Sheehan

Marketing Consultant Mark Sutcliffe (Make My Mark)
Literary Manager Christopher Hurrell
Head Trainer - Corporate Training Nicholas Flanagan
Production Manager Miles Thomas
Front-of-House Manager Matthew Lilley
Front-of-House Supervisors Nick Terrell & Kerry-A Staker-Matthews
Publicist Lara Raymond
Graphic Designer Jeremy Saunders
Web Designer Julian Oppen (Full Cream Media)
Education Consultant Dr Wendy Michaels

Griffin Donors

Income from Griffin activities covers less than 50% of Griffin's operating costs – leaving an ever increasing gap fo to fill through government funding, sponsorship and philanthropy. Your support helps us bridge the gap and keep tic prices affordable and our programs working at their best. To make a donation contact Griffin on 9332 1052 or don online on the Griffin website www.griffintheatre.com.au.

GUARDIAN ($10,000+)
Anonymous x 2
The Late Lady Nancy Fairfax OBE
The Petre Foundation

GOLD ($5000 - $9999)
RebelStudio Pty Limited
Regents Court Hotel

SILVER ($2500 - $4999)
Richard Cottrell
Hugh Jackman & Deborra-Lee Furness
Geoff & Wendy Simpson
Joseph Skrzynski AM & Ros Horin

BRONZE ($1000 - $2499)
Anonymous
Collider
Deborah Balderstone
Michael Bradley
Michael Choong & Harold Melnick
Peter Graves
Peter Keel
Jennifer Ledgar & Bob Lim
Sarah Longes
Chris & Fran Roberts
Dr Rodney F. Seaborn AO OBE

ASSOCIATE ($500 - $999)
Antoinette Albert
Gil Appleton
The Grumley Family
Macgowan films
Parsons Family Trust

Rod Phillips
Mrs Betty J Raghavan
Rebel Studio Pty Ltd
Annabel Ritchie
Kim Williams AM

FRIEND ($100 - $499)
Steven Alward & Mark Wakely
Carl Andrew
Anonymous x 2
Gregory Ashton
Rob Brookman & Verity Laughton
Denise and Neil Buchanan
Wendy Buswell
Terence Clarke
Victor Cohen
John Crocker
D.W. Knox & Partners
Di Davis
Victoria Doidge
Jo Dyer
Rosalind Fischl
Nicky Gluyas
HLA Management Pty Ltd
Janet Heffernan
Mary & John Holt
Beverley Johnson
Gloria Jones
Geoffrey Lack
David Lieberman
Ian Marsh
Neville Mitchell
Kate O'Brien
Brian & Lyn Oliver
Betty Raghavan

Arahni Sont
Ross Steele AM
Gary Sullivan
Roz Tarszisz
John Thacker
David Thomson
Robyn Tooth
Julie Wyer
Vera Zukerman

CONTRIBUTOR (<$100)
Robyn Ayres
Gary Balzola
Bronwen Bassett
Jane Bridge
Jason Catlett
Sharan Daly
Catherine Duggan
Gemma Edgar
Mrs R Espie
Elizabeth Evatt
Michael Eyers
Colin Fainberg
Belinda Firmstone
William Franken
Emily Hale
Noelene Hall
Norman Hams
Belinda Hazelton
Kevin Hewitt
Gary Hodson
Marianne Hoeg
Barbara Holmes
Joan Humphreys
Peter Ikin

Hazel Kelly
Mary Lawson
Stephanie Lawson
Caroline Le Plastrier
Jean Prouvaire
Christine Lozano
Sacha Macansh
Ruth Marshall
Andrew McMillan
Frances Milat
Tom Milligan
Peter Noble
Doreen Payne
Dianne Pearson
Fiona Press
Ann Proudfoot
Jean Prouvaire
Warren Riolo
Catherine Rothery
Kay Ryan
Sharon Shapiro
Nancy Squires
Dr Leigh Sutherland
Helen Thompson
Beris Tomkins
Mark and Lynn Trainor
Douglas Trengrove
Irma Trnka
Jennifer Turnbull
Daniel Vucetich
David Wallace
Elizabeth Webb
Anna Zysk

2008 Griffin Partners

Principal Sponsor
PKF
Chartered Accountants & Business Advisers

Venture Partner
gadens lawyers

Production Partner
holding redlich

Company Partners
blakehurst technology
CURRENCY PRESS — The performing arts publisher — www.currency.com.au
THE FEAROCIOUS FEED
fullcream media
REGENTS COURT HOTEL
SEABORN BROUGHTON & WALFORD FOUNDATION
SIGNWAVE NEWTOWN
TYRRELL'S WINES
UNSW SCHOOL OF MEDIA, FILM AND THEATRE
THE VICTORIA ROOM

Artistic Partners
ARTS ON TOUR NSW
apa arts projects AUSTRALIA
HotHouse Theatre
nowyesnow
Performing Lines
Riverside

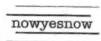

Media Partner
Time Out Sydney

Philanthropic Partners
COPYRIGHT AGENCY LIMITED
EQUITY TRUSTEES FOUNDATION
THE MALCOLM ROBERTSON FOUNDATION

Honorary Auditors
Rosenfeld, Kant & Co.

SBW Stables Theatre Owned By
SBW Foundation (Seaborn Broughton & Walford Foundation)

Government Partners
Australian Government
arts nsw
CITY OF SYDNEY
Australian Government — Playing Australia

Griffin is grateful to the UNSW School of English Media and Performing Arts for its ongoing rehearsal support.

Griffin Theatre is assisted by the Australian Government through the Australia Council, its arts funding and advisory body; and the NSW Government through Arts NSW.

Griffin acknowledges the generosity of the Seaborn Broughton and Walford Foundation in allowing it, since 1986, the use of the SBW Stables Theatre rent free, less outgoings.

...proudly supporting the Griffin Theatre's
Playwright Residency...

gadens
lawyers